GROWING PAINS

MY JOURNEY OF SELF DISCOVERY

By: Hidden Diamond 💎

ISBN: 978-1-956884-30-2

Contributing Editor: All services completed by Imprint Productions, Inc. Cover Design: All services completed by Imprint Productions, Inc. Printed in the United States of America. Published by Imprint Productions, Inc.

First Edition 2024

Contact: info@imprintproductionsinc.com

Visit Us: www.imprintproductionsinc.com

DEDICATION

This book is dedicated to all the brokenhearted people seeking
healing. Jesus Christ can heal you and
turn your pain into purpose.

Try Jesus. He is waiting for you.

In Loving Memory of My Amazing Parents

Stephanie Smith   &   Charlie Hardnett

# INTRODUCTION

My growing pains began when I was about six years old.
My mother had recently brought a new boyfriend home to live
with us. He was smart, handsome, and fun to be around. But he
was also a drug addict and a mean drunk. Despite his flaws, he was
very good to us. My two brothers at the time, and I had different
fathers. Their father was not active in their lives; however, my
father was a big part of my life. For that, I was grateful. My mom's
boyfriend played the role of stepfather well and we loved him. One
day my father was scheduled to pick me up and take me to the zoo.
I waited the entire day, but when the sun began to set I knew he
wasn't coming. I was scared because I didn't know what happened
to him. For whatever reason, my mom did not have a telephone
number for him. In my young mind, I thought that I had did
something wrong, or that something happened to him. As time
went by, I realized that I wouldn't see my father again, but at least
I had a good stepfather. My admiration for him would be short
lived. As I stated earlier, our new stepfather was an addict and a
mean drunk. One Friday evening my mother was cooking fish and
fries for dinner for us, and he came home high. He accused her of
cheating on him in "his" house because the house smelled like fish.
He beat her so bad that she was barely recognizable. My brothers
and I were terrified, fearful, and confused. Our new "stepfather"

was a wrathful monster, and for the next five years we would have to endure watching our mother be beaten.

From that day forward, our lives became a living hell. We were in constant fear, afraid to leave our mother in the house alone, afraid that our mom would say the wrong thing. He never hit us, but with every blow he gave our mom, it felt like he did. In a drunken rage, he would kick in our front door, if our mom locked him out. At this point, I became resentful to my father. It's been almost three years now since that faithful day that he stood me up with no explanation. I'm his child. How could he allow me to live like this? How could he leave me when I needed him the most? I was hopeless and afraid. We were absent from school allot, but our grades were excellent. I made the honor roll every year, and my oldest brother was a great football player. None of our teachers knew what was happening at home. We knew that if we told them, they would take us from our mother. So, we suffered in silence.

This silence spread like a disease in every area of our lives. We didn't dare speak our true feelings about how we were feeling inside. We just coped with it. Depression and suicidal thoughts became my solace. Every day I thought about killing myself. I was in the middle of a whirlwind not of my making, and I wanted out. After a while, I became angry with my mother. I would ask her time and time again why she allowed this to happen to us. She would say that she didn't know. I felt like my mom chose her boyfriend over us, and I felt abandoned and lonely. At 12 years old

I decided that I had enough! It was time to leave this miserable life. I locked myself in the bathroom, took a bottle of pills, poured some in my hand, swallowed them, and waited to either pass out or die.

As I laid on the floor and waited, I heard an audible voice say, "What would your mother do if she found you in here dead" The thought never crossed my mind! She was already going through so much; this would break her, but what about me! What about her lifestyle making "me" want to die? At that moment, I realized that I had to live. I had to live for my mother. I tried to regurgitate, but it wouldn't come up. That night I was afraid that I would die in my sleep, so I stayed up until I couldn't stay awake anymore. The next morning it was like I never took a handful of pills. No cramps, no drowsiness. Nothing. I realize now that the voice I heard speaking to me, was the voice of GOD. As a side note, I must say that I have to say "We" while giving this testimony, because "we" literally went through it together. Yes, it impacted us differently but "we", my mom, my older brother, middle brother, and I weathered this storm together. Our family abandoned us when my mom refused to leave the abusive relationship. We had no support, outlet, or a place of refuge.

My grandfather gave us food when there was no money to buy any, but beyond that, nothing. We were on our own, and we had to grow up and grow up fast. Our childhood was bittersweet, but we knew that life was not what we saw on TV. After five long years of abuse, and two baby brothers added to our family, my mother had finally had enough. She finally kicked him out, and he stayed out. We were relieved, but paranoid. We didn't know what to expect. So we lived one day at a time until we were able to move on. We didn't talk about the storm we just went through it. We just tried to live our lives as best we could. My childhood had molded my perception of men, love, life and GOD. At the time, I didn't believe in GOD. I didn't believe that HE would allow children to live this way. We lived in the projects at the time, and there was so much homelessness and despair, that I just couldn't see HIM in it.

This line of thinking followed me into my teenage years and adulthood. My attitude was to live, like there were no consequences to follow. In my "living" I found out that I was really "dying". I was broken, and all of the partying and drinking, couldn't take away the pain. Silently, I was suicidal, I had no sense of self-worth, or value, my self-esteem was nonexistent, I felt abandoned and rejected. I felt like I wasn't good enough to be loved, so I did like any broken person would do; I tried to "make" men love me. I thought if I gave them my body, money, time and support, that men would see my value and want to stay in my life. The TV and magazines said that this was how to do it, but it didn't work for me. It left me even more empty, broken, and shallow. By age 15, I was so desperate for love and acceptance, that the pain was too much to bare. My oldest brothers' girlfriend, who is now his wife, asked us to go to church with her. We (my oldest brother and I), started going to church. The experience was wonderful. We gave our lives to Christ, joined her church, got baptized and we were on our way to walking out our salvation. It was short lived. Eventually we stopped attending church, and we were back doing what we wanted to do.

Finally, by age 21, I thought I had found the answer to all my problems! This guy was so handsome that I felt like it was an honor that he chose me to be his woman! He understood me, and we would laugh, talk, and share our dreams and plan for a great future together. It didn't matter that he was about to get out of jail and was down on his luck and needed help. I had his back. That's what a good woman do for her man right? What a sad fairytale that I actually believed would come true. Well, it never happened. We broke up. To be honest, this time I wasn't broken up about it.

As time went by, I realized that he wasn't the person that he appeared to be. I was a naïve pawn, a means for him to establish himself once we got out of jail. When he did, that was it. A little later, I moved into my first apartment and was struggling a little bit. He calls me out the blue and wants to stop by. I gave him my address, and it was a pleasant visit, up until I asked him to help me out a little bit. To my surprise, he told me no. I was shocked, broken and felt like a real fool. I told him thanks anyway and enjoy the rest of his night. After he left, this strong spirit of suicide came over me.

I burst into a sweat and thought about getting a knife to cut my wrist. This time, I couldn't shake it off, this time, I was afraid that I would really follow through with what the voices were telling me to do. I didn't know what to do. So, I went into my bedroom and shut the door. I kneeled down on the side of my bed and reintroduced myself to GOD. I told HIM that I needed HIM to come into my life. That I was scared that if HE didn't help me that I would kill myself. I repented of all my sins, and I poured out my heart unto HIM. After I prayed and cried for about two hours, I finally went to bed, and I slept like a baby. From that day forward, my journey with the LORD began. Almost overnight, the desire for sex, the suicidal thoughts, and the brokenness was gone. No longer did I need a man, I had found "THE MAN" which was Jesus Christ. I stopped searching for men to define who I was, and allowed GOD to reveal to me who I was. For the first time since I was thirteen years old, I didn't have a man in my life, and it felt really good. The LORD became my FATHER and my GOD. HE became everything that I needed. HE provided, HE affirmed, HE chastised, HE encouraged, HE revealed and revealed me to myself. I now know that my source of life does not come from men, but a source that is eternal in Christ Jesus. I no longer thirst for love but am truly filled and whole.

During my journey of healing, the LORD allowed me to make peace with my parents and my moms' ex-boyfriend. My mother and I finally talked about what happened. She said that she felt like being with him was the only way she knew to take care of us. His income contributed to our wellbeing. She said she hardly remember the physical abuse, but the verbal abuse she did. My mother encouraged me to learn from her mistakes and to make better decisions. Eventually, she received Jesus Christ as LORD and Savior. She was baptized and filled with the Holy Spirit. GOD healed her mind and gave her peace from her hard life.

On September 14, 2016, at the tender age of 54, my mother went home to be with the LORD. I miss her more with each passing day, but I believe that because she was a soldier to the very end of her life, she deserves her rest. It's so funny how I never connected the source of my brokenness to the day my father left my life at six years old. But GOD did. I was able to reconnect with him after he and his wife were in a horrible car accident. Although my father never gave me an explanation for his actions, while on his death bed we forgave one another, and on June 26, 2023, after his 73rd birthday, he went home to be with the LORD.

My parents sudden passings, helped me to understand in a greater way the power of pain. Pain was not designed to break us down, but an instrument used by GOD to build us up into the image of HIS son Jesus Christ! Without pain, I wouldn't have given my life to the LORD. Without pain, I wouldn't know my true identity which is in Christ Jesus. Without pain, I wouldn't know that the Word of GOD is real and has the power to deliver and heal us from our hurts, habits and hang ups. Most importantly, without pain, I wouldn't know my purpose in life. For this reason, the LORD inspired me to write this book for the next generation of young believers. Your pain has purpose and if you will allow GOD to walk you through this process you will come out victorious.

HIS thoughts are not our thoughts, and HIS ways are not our ways (Isaiah 55:8-9), but by faith as believers in Jesus Christ, we are encouraged to believe that GOD has the power to make us better, not bitter. This collection of poems tells my story of growing pains and allowing GOD to turn it into purpose. I pray as you read through these poems, that GOD will move mightily through your heart, and bring you to a place of hope and peace. You may be experiencing the darkest hours of your life. Just know that GOD loves you and is with you every step of the way. Be encouraged, trust GOD, be thankful for everything HE has done for you thus far in your life. Above all, I pray that you change your perspective about your growing pains, believing that in the end GOD has a great purpose and an amazing future instore for you!

Be Encouraged, Be Excited, and Be Victorious
Hidden Diamond

Acknowledgements

To my LORD and Savior Jesus Christ, tears of joy spring to my eyes whenever I think of your luv, patience, and goodness towards me. Thank you for saving my life and allowing me to experience new life in you. I pray that when you search my heart, you will see the sincerity of my words. I'm grateful to call you Father and GOD. I luv you.

To my family, we have gone through so much, but through it all GOD has sustained us. I'm so excited to see what HE has in store for us. Luv You all. To my best friend Dishonia, you have seen me at my worst. Yet through it all, you never stopped supporting me. Thank you for 20+ years of friendship. Luv you Sis.

To my kingdom partner Idris. Thank you for being such an inspiration and a blessing in my life. Our path to purpose and destiny has not been easy, but I thank GOD for HIS transformative power molding us into HIS image. Let GOD be glorified through our journey!

To my amazing godparents, Kenny and Alisa Carpenter, I'm so blessed to have you both in my life! Your luv, support, and encouragement has kept me during my journey. Thank you for standing in the gap during the most difficult times of my life. To Sweet Pea, thanks for believing in me, even when I didn't believe in myself. Your friendship and guidance has kept me out of a lot of trouble! LOL. BUT GOD! Luv you.

John, through our many ups and downs, I can honestly say that I'm grateful to call you friend. Thanks for always having my back.

To my friend and powerful prayer warrior in the LORD Ree, through many storms, you have prayed me and my family through. For many years we have laughed, cried, and encouraged each other in the LORD.

Sometimes over some good Chinese food! Thank you for your friendship, wisdom, knowledge and luv. Luv ya Sis.

To my church family Peace Baptist Church in Decatur, GA you have truly been a blessing! Thank you so much for your prayers and support.

To Daphne King, Kimberly Jackson, Cheryl Blandon and Daphne Jackson thank you so much for taking the time to review and provide your honest feedback on this book. Thank you for your luv and support. To Prophetess Bella, wow what an amazing Woman of GOD. Thank you for your willingness to use your natural and spiritual gifts, to be such a blessing in my life. May GOD use you mightily for HIS glory.

My new friend and sister in Christ Candance, thanks for being such a breath of fresh air. Thank you for imparting wisdom, perspective, and correction into my life. May GOD bless you in this new season of your life.

Finally, to my readers, thank you so much for taking the time to purchase and read this book. I pray that it blesses and inspire you to come out of your hidden places of darkness, brokenness, and pain, into the marvelous, healing light of our LORD & Savior Jesus Christ.

Blessings,

Hidden Diamond

REFLECTION

When I look into the mirror, what do I see?

A reflection of a woman redeemed staring back at me

I wasn't born into this reflection, I was created into it

Like a Diamond hidden deep in the earth, and no one

could get to it

No one could see the transformation taking place

People walked by and didn't hear my cry, yet GOD granted me

grace

The Lord drew me out of the darkness so that I could shine

Now understanding the necessity of being hidden, so the glory

wouldn't be mine

A true reflection of your glory, that's what you created me to be

The beauty of our Eternal GOD is being revealed in me.

WORDS OF WISDOM
REFLECTION

As believers in Jesus Christ, we are called to reflect the character of GOD in the earth. Not only for unbelievers but also for ourselves. We owe it to GOD to be the best version of ourselves that HE knows we are capable of being. Many of us have faced challenges that have hindered us from seeing GOD and ourselves the way HE does. That's why it's so important to have a personal relationship with GOD so that HE can reveal the amazing person you are created and destined to be. Apart from Christ, you can do nothing, but in HIM you can do all things (See Philippians 4:13). The journey may not be easy but know that HE is with you every step of the way.

LAY IT ON THE ALTAR

How can you expect me

to let go of all the cruel things he did to me?

My heart shattered in a million pieces in my hands

Never expecting it to be put back together again

Yet you say lay it on the altar as an offering to you

But if I let this go, who does the power belong to?

The one that stripped me of my right to live?

Yet you tell me that I have the power to forgive?

Lay it on the altar you say to me

I can give you a new heart if you would only trust Me

To give you beauty for ashes as you tell your story

Of how I made you whole, and I will get all the Glory

WORDS OF WISDOM

LAY IT ON THE ALTAR

Can I be honest? Sometimes, forgiving those who have hurt or offended us can be difficult, but not impossible! The word of GOD encourages us…. "I can do all things through Christ which strengthens me" (Philippians 4:13).

When you forgive, it is not for the other person, but for "you". How? Because it's GOD's way for "you" to be free from the pain! When you truly forgive, the enemy can no longer use that emotional pain as a weapon to hurt you, through painful memories, negative thoughts, and behaviors.

GOD through his grace and mercy, can use the very thing that the enemy meant to hurt and harm you, and make you an overcomer of it! GOD has granted us this power through HIS Son Jesus Christ. He overcame all the works of the enemy. It's through HIM that we can face our pain and be healed. It's through HIM that we can forgive those who have hurt or offended us. It's through HIM that we are given the opportunity to have a new life, and freedom from our past.

Make the decision today to turn your pain into power, by laying your broken heart on the altar of the LORD in prayer. Allow HIM to give you a new beginning, and beauty for ashes.

CANDY JAR

Like a candy jar, you have filled me with sweet things

Each piece of candy is like a testimony of the joy you bring

What was once bitter to taste, you have made so sweet

Making each piece of candy so dear to me

No longer ashamed, I joyfully share

These tasty treats with others, to show that I care

I will carry this jar wherever I go

As a memento of your goodness, and how you love me so

WORDS OF WISDOM
CANDY JAR

According to Google Dictionary, the word "Testimony" is defined as "Evidence or proof provided by the existence or appearance of something". When we face life challenges and overcome them, we are showing proof that GOD IS REAL! We share this proof or evidence by sharing our testimonies with others.

Since I began my journey with the LORD Jesus Christ 16 years ago, I have been granted grace to face many challenges. However, with each storm, I have come to know that GOD is real. I have been placed in impossible situations and could see no way out of them. BUT GOD! Each challenge I've faced and endured in HIS strength, and not my own, has allowed me to know the truth of HIS word, and its many promises. Each storm has revealed character defects, that GOD wanted me to be set free from. Though the experiences were painful, I can now thank GOD for them.

Allow GOD to give you a testimony, so you can discover who HE is for yourself and share it with the world. It's when we are in the darkest hours of our lives, that we truly see the truth and light of GOD. When we discover this truth, and GOD grants us the grace of knowing HIM for ourselves, the enemy can't take the reality of HIS existence away from us. Why not? Because like a candy jar, we carry the proof, (our testimonies) in our hearts with us always.

THE SWEETEST THING

It was the sweetest thing for me to hear

That you were willing to sacrifice what you held so dear

For a world that rebelled, and turned its back on you

Yet you thought we were worth saving and extending Your grace to

You sent your Son in spite of it all

To redeem us from the consequences of the fall

To be vessels of your glory, and to minister unto you

For that's the purpose of our existence, and what we were created to do

I rejoice, as my soul begins to sing

At the manifestation of your love, and the eternal

joy that it brings

TESTIMONY

THE SWEETEST THING

My middle school was a part of the Big Brothers, Big Sisters Organization, a non-profit mentorship program for children. I was assigned a "Big Sister" and in GOD's divine plan, she was the First Lady of a community church! I attended my first church service at 12 years old, and for the very first time, I heard the Gospel of Jesus Christ preached. I didn't have a clue about what was being said, but my momma and "big sister" encouraged us (me and my oldest brother) to keep attending.

By age 13 my family and I moved to another side of town, and I stopped attending church. I was a teenager and wanted to experience "life". What I thought was "living" was really "recklessness", but GOD granted me grace.

Years later, one faithful evening the enemy attacked my mind with suicidal thoughts. Little did I know that the seed (The Word of GOD) was already planted in my spirit from 12 years old. The Word of GOD rose up in my spirit and reminded me that

GOD would fight my battles. I repented for my rebellion and re-dedicated my life back to GOD.

It was the sweetest thing for me to hear the Voice of GOD reminding me that evening, that HE IS REAL! No matter how far away we are from HIS original plan for our lives, HIS love pleads for us to come back to HIM. It's even sweeter that HE knew from the very beginning that we would make mistakes, stumble, and sometimes fall on our journey with HIM. Nevertheless, HE still sent HIS only begotten Son, Jesus Christ of Nazareth, to die for our sins, so that we could live in eternity with HIM. How Sweet is our Heavenly Father!

PSALMS 91

(New King James Version)

He who dwells in the secret place of the Most High shall abide under the shadow of the Almighty.

I will say of the Lord, "He is my refuge and my fortress; My God, in Him I will trust."

Surely, He shall deliver you from the snare of the fowler, and from the perilous pestilence.

He shall cover you with His feathers, and under His wings, you shall take refuge.

His truth shall be your shield and buckler.

You shall not be afraid of the terror by night, nor of the arrow that flies by day,

Nor of the pestilence that walks in darkness, nor of the destruction that lays waste at noonday.

A thousand may fall at your side, and ten thousand at your right hand, but it shall not come near you.

Only with your eyes shall you look and see the reward of the wicked.

Because you have made the Lord, who is my refuge, even the Most High, your dwelling place,

No evil shall befall you, nor shall any plague come near your dwelling.

For He shall give His angels charge over you, to keep you in all your ways.

In their hands, they shall bear you up, lest you dash your foot against a stone.

You shall tread upon the lion and the cobra, the young lion, and the serpent you shall trample underfoot.

Because he has set his love upon Me, therefore I will deliver him; I will set him on high because he has known My name.

He shall call upon Me, and I will answer him; I will be with him in trouble.

I will deliver him and honor him.

With long life, I will satisfy him and show him My salvation.

TESTIMONY

PSALMS 91

For 15 years, I worked at a correctional facility for men, in Atlanta, GA. Every day I made it home alive is GOD's grace and protection. That's why every morning I read and declare Psalms 91 over my life, to remind GOD of what HE said about protecting me. Since I have made Psalms 91 a part of my daily devotion time with the LORD, I'm convinced that GOD is with me, and there is no reason to fear!

Throughout my journey with the LORD, I have witnessed the truth of Psalms 91 in action, and it gives me a Holy Fear and Reverence of GOD and HIS word. Whenever I recognize the enemy trying to stir up fear in my heart, I cast his lies down in the Mighty Name of Jesus! I declare Psalms 91, to remind the enemy that I abide in GOD, and not his lies. My peace, joy, rest, and protection are in the Mighty

hands of GOD. Let this blessed assurance be with you

my brothers and sisters always. FAITH OVER FEAR.

AMEN.

BETTER, NOT BITTER

Be silent devil! How dare you try to intimidate me

You thought that when the LORD called my momma

home you would break me

My heart shattered and confusion surrounded me

Temptation to fall back into a world that was no longer

for me

Your plan was to take my life and I forever lose my soul

But I'm better, not bitter

You thought that I would let go of HIS hand

To walk back into the world, yep that was your plan

To flood my emotions with doubt about GOD's perfect

plan

But I'm better, not bitter

Be silent devil! I shouted in agony

I will not forfeit my destiny

I'll praise my GOD with every breath in me

Until my tears dry up, and I can truly see

The beauty for ashes GOD will soon give me

NO DEVIL, I'm Better, Not Bitter

TESTIMONY

BETTER, NOT BITTER

My amazing mother, Stephanie Parks-Smith passed away suddenly on September 14, 2016, at the tender age of 54. My mother was my best friend and a true example of GOD's sustaining power. She was a very loving and affectionate woman and instilled the same attributes into me and my four brothers. She wasn't a perfect woman, and was honest enough to admit it, but she was the perfect vessel to mold and guide me and my brothers, for the purposes GOD has for our lives. I'm grateful to GOD that before HE called her home, that she was saved, baptized, and filled with HIS Spirit. Her soul has a place with HIM in heaven, and that gives me comfort.

As I reflect on that season of my life, I believe that the Holy Spirit was teaching me how to surrender. Everything that I was going through during that time was above my pay grade. Meaning that I had no control or could voice a favorable opinion to bring my mom back.

Everything I was going through was in the mighty hands of GOD, and I could NOT control HIM. All I could do was surrender. It was only when I began to ask the LORD to help me to surrender, that the depression that attempted to overtake me lifted, and the peace of GOD that surpasses all understanding, found a place in my heart. No, I couldn't bring my mom back, and I couldn't change the spiral downfall in my life that took place proceeding her passing, but GOD changed me in spite of it all.

I praise GOD for allowing me to experience first-hand the power of prayer. Oftentimes, we don't always see or experience the immediate results from it, but GOD in HIS grace and mercy towards me, allowed me to "feel" in my spirit, the words of life being imparted within me. I'm so grateful for the Prayer Ministry at my church because they also share in the belief that prayer is the key to releasing GOD's power into the earth and our circumstances. Now that GOD has brought me over, I can honestly say and testify, that GOD's word is real. HE promises us in HIS word that HE would keep us from falling. (See Jude 1:24), and I can testify that it's true! HE kept me in my darkest hours from the hands of the enemy. HE lifted me up in my spirit and renewed my mind. In the midst of my pain and sorrow, HE made me BETTER, NOT BITTER!

Dear God,

Can I be honest with you? I don't understand! I don't understand why you created me, or what my purpose on this earth is. Things are getting crazy down here, and your word regarding your return is quickly unfolding. Yet, you said in your word, that all things are working for our good. How will my sufferings make a positive difference in this world? I just don't understand.

Every day is a struggle, Father. To walk in love, and to live a holy life before you. The temptation of sin is sometimes difficult to resist LORD, and sometimes I fall short of your glory. Please forgive me. Help me to walk out this journey with you. Help me to recognize the schemes of the enemy, so that I can avoid his traps, or give me strength to fight the good fight of faith. Help me to believe your word, even if I don't see immediate manifestations of it. Help me to smile in the faces of my enemies, and not cry before them. Simply put, I need you, and there is no way I can live without you. Help me.

Love Your Daughter,

Hidden Diamond

My Precious Daughter,

I'm so proud of you! Why? Because you finally understand that I AM your Source. Only I can answer the questions of your heart. Only I can reveal to you your purpose and destiny. For many years you lived your life independent of me. Yet I have loved you in spite of. I have protected you and preserved your life for such a time as this.

Before you came into this world, I knew you. I created you just the way I wanted you to be, in the country you are born in, and the family you are a part of. Your life may not be ideal in your sight, but your life was never created for you, but for me to be glorified through it. Yes, my daughter you have experienced pain, and trauma, and have cried many tears; however, I have promised and will not rescind, that all things are working for your good. Can you trust me to turn your pain, frustration, and tears into power? Can you trust me to

lead and guide you in your journey with me? Will you believe me when I say that I will never leave you nor forsake you? My daughter, be at peace. For your thoughts are not my thoughts and your ways are not my ways. Trust me, and I will reveal to you MY plans for your life.

My daughter, it is time for my children to rise up. Rise up and see that the enemy is already defeated! Do not be afraid of the darkness that is spreading like wildfire upon the earth. For My light and glory shine brightest in darkness. Rise up in your spirit, and see as I see, hear as I hear, and become confident in who I AM. I AM the Lord of Host, and My army is ready to destroy all of the works of the enemy. Only Believe. Believe in My word, and I will give you power through the Holy

Spirit, to overcome the works of the enemy. No weapon formed against you shall prosper, Only Believe!

As I bring this letter to a close, I have a request; tell my sons and daughters all around the world that I love them. Tell them that no matter how far away they are from My will for their lives and my love for them has not changed. Tell them to repent, and to come back to Me, and I will receive them with open arms. The blood of My SON has already paid the price for their sins. There is no shame or condemnation in Me. Only grace and mercy. Tell My children that I'm coming quickly, and to make themselves ready. Be strong and hold fast to My word.

Loving You Now & Forever More,

Abba

THIRSTY

As the deer pants for the water brooks, so pants my soul for You, O GOD. My soul thirst for GOD, for the living GOD: when shall I come and appear before GOD? [1]

My soul is all dried up from the heat of the battle, in the wilderness do I cry out to thee.

My Father, My GOD hear my plea

I'm thirsty **LORD GOD**, send your living water to me

Refresh my soul, renew my strength, let my sorrow turn into joy

My enemies surround me on all sides, but there's no fight left in me

Send your living water My **LORD**, My **GOD** send your living water

I'm thirsty

Psalms 42: 1-2 (New Kings James Version Bible)

TESTIMONY

THIRSTY

During one particular season of my life, I was diligently seeking the LORD in prayer and supplication, for clarity and guidance about some challenges I was facing, but GOD was silent. I didn't understand at the time, that GOD was creating a thirst and hunger for HIM in my spirit. In essence, HE was teaching me how to wait for HIM.

Isaiah 40:31 says, "But they that wait upon the LORD shall renew their strength, they shall mount up with wings as eagles; they shall run, and not be weary; and they shall walk, and not faint. (KJV)

As a child of GOD, learning how to wait on HIM is one of the most difficult yet rewarding lessons I had to learn. Because I'm human, I have a natural desire to always be in control of my own life and circumstances. However, this way of thinking is contrary to the will and ways of GOD. When I re-dedicated my life to the LORD, I gave HIM permission to take control of my life. As a result of my commitment to the LORD, an exchange had to take place. I had to release my human desires and reasonings and receive the Fruit of HIS Spirit, (love, joy, peace, long-suffering, gentleness, goodness, faith, meekness, and temperance). This exchange was frustrating and painful, yet GOD was more than able to see me through.

I want to encourage you my brothers and sisters to allow the LORD to take you through this process. In doing so, HE will stir up a thirst and a hunger for HIS presence deep within your spirit. Allow HIM to manifest HIS Glory through you. You won't regret it.

THE TRUE WORSHIPPER

I'm a true worshipper and I do not fear

The stares of the onlookers as I enter near

HIS throne of grace, mercy, and truth

To sing a song of praise for all the amazing things that you do

It's ok for them to watch, let this worship bless them too

Rejoicing in the day when we all will worship HIM in Spirit and in Truth

Standing in HIS presence, it's an audience of ONE

My inner man must worship HIM for all HE has done

HIS Life saved me, and HIS blood redeemed me

My heart knows the transformation, that's why I worship HIM so freely

With tears of joy running down my face

I thank HIM for giving me the strength to continue in this race

To finish strong and glorify HIM all the days of my life

And that my worship would be true, and forever pleasing in your sight

TESTIMONY

THE TRUE WORSHIPPER

I am a worshipper, and I have an audience of One.
Sometimes my worship is gentle and in the beauty of
holiness. Other times it's loud, spontaneous, and energetic.
Either way, GOD is worthy to be praised and adored.

In my opinion, worship is personal, and there is no right or
wrong way to do it. As long as it's in Spirit and in truth.
GOD wants our worship to be authentic. HE is the one that
searches our hearts to see if it's true. Whether we worship
HIM through song, dance, poetry, or however the Holy
Spirit leads us, be authentic. Let it be pleasing in HIS sight,
and not in the sight of man. Allow your worship to bring
glory to HIS Mighty name. "Let everything that has breath
praise the LORD" (Psalms 150:6KJV)

SLAVE

I was your slave, and you wanted me to be

Blinded by lust and deception you mastered me

But the Blood of Jesus Christ has set me free

It's time for you to let me go

My ears longed to hear your beautiful lies

Killing me softly you buried me alive

A slave to sin and imprisoned in my mind

It's time for you to let me go

The word of GOD declares it to be,

That whom the Son sets free is truly free indeed[2]

The shackles are destroyed and no longer bind me,

To yesterday's failures and the pain caused by the enemy

I've been emancipated, Christ paid the cost

And has given me the power to regain everything I have lost

A woman redeemed, that's now who I am

Forever grateful for the BLOOD OF THE LAMB

John 8: 36 (New King James Version)

TESTIMONY

SLAVE

Before I re-dedicated my life to Christ, I knew that I had to get my life together, but I didn't know how. It was as if there was an invisible chain wrapped around me that kept me enslaved to sin. I wanted to change the direction of my life, and I knew that there was more to me and the way I was living. I just couldn't seem to break free from sin.

Now that I have totally surrendered my life to the Lord Jesus Christ, I now understand what real freedom and liberty is. It's only by the power of the Holy Spirit, that we are truly set free from the enslavement of sin. The word of GOD declares in Zechariah 4:6

"….. Not by might, nor by power, but by my spirit, saith the LORD of hosts".

We are NEVER so far gone in sin that GOD can't reach HIS powerful hands down and bring us out of it! HE CAN, AND HE WILL!

Yes, we are human, and we will sometimes make mistakes. Repent, and keep striving to become the person GOD has created you to be. Put your faith and trust in GOD, and HE will bring you to a place of VICTORY!

SHOUT IN VICTORY

Yes, I shout in victory

Because GOD saw fit to send HIS Son to Cavalry

Nailed to the cross was my pain and sins

Granting me the right to be born again

The blood HE shed made it possible for me

To lift up my head and believe that I'm somebody.

Free from my past, now I can truly see

The Victory of the cross, and my future before me

TESTIMONY

SHOUT IN VICTORY

I remember at the tender age of 12 struggling with suicidal thoughts. Years later at 21 years old, the thoughts and desires suddenly came upon me, and I couldn't shake off the emotions and urges. This time, I was afraid that I would actually harm myself. I didn't know what to do. Suddenly, a voice rose up in my spirit, reminding me that GOD would fight my battles. I went into my bedroom and shut the door. I kneeled down on the side of my bed and rededicated my life to Jesus Christ. I told HIM that I needed HIM to come into my life, that I was scared that if HE didn't help me, I would harm myself. I repented of all my sins, and I poured out my heart to HIM. After I prayed and cried for about two hours, I finally went to bed, and I slept like a baby.

From that day forward, my journey with the LORD began. Almost overnight, the suicidal thoughts, the brokenness, and pain were gone. The LORD became my FATHER and my GOD. HE became everything that I needed in my life. HE provided, affirmed, chastised, encouraged, revealed, and exposed me to myself. He set me free in ways that I can't begin to express. I'm no longer a slave to the negative emotions and snares of the enemy, but free. Free to be the woman that GOD created me to be. Now I can shout in victory because I know that no matter what battle comes my way, I'm persuaded that GOD is fighting for me! HALLELUJAH!

CAVALRY'S SONG

The sweetest song is being sung

From a place called Calvary where Victory reigns

Be still my soul and be attentive

For the words of this song are on a mission

To reclaim what was lost and give it back to you

For the blood of Jesus is singing a new song, and is crying out for you

A new covenant has been established, let us rejoice and be true

To Cavalry's Song, the way that leads to life anew

WORDS OF WISDOM

CAVALRY'S SONG

I was reading and meditating on the book of Hebrews when I came to this scripture that says…

"By faith Abel offered to GOD a more excellent sacrifice than Cain, through which he obtained witness that he was righteous, GOD testifying of his gifts: and through it, he being dead still speaks." Hebrews 11:4, (NKJV)

How much so the Sacrifice of Christ! If the place of sacrifice for Abel is still speaking to GOD, how much so is Cavalry? The ultimate place of sacrifice where the enemies of GOD were defeated, and humanity redeemed. The place where a new and better covenant was made with GOD and HIS people. Victory truly reigns on Calvary! HALLELUJAH.

PSALMS 23

(New King James Version Bible)

The Lord is my shepherd; I shall not want.

He makes me to lie down in green pastures; he leads me beside the still waters.

He restores my soul; he leads me on the paths of righteousness

For His name's sake.

Yea, though I walk through the valley of the shadow of death,

I will fear no evil; for You are with me; Your rod and Your staff, they comfort me.

You prepare a table before me in the presence of my enemies; you anoint my head with oil; My cup runs over.

Surely goodness and mercy shall follow me all the days of my life.

And I will dwell in the house of the Lord Forever.

TESTIMONY

PSALMS 23

(New King James Version)

At the leading of the Holy Spirit, I began a monthly prayer service at an active senior living home. I truly enjoy serving the senior citizens. In my opinion, they are living witnesses of GOD's grace, mercy, and sustaining power. They prove that in spite of the many challenges they have faced in their lifetimes, GOD can still give you joy and peace and that His unrelentless love towards us is eternal.

During one of my monthly visits, I asked the participants if they had a gospel song that they wanted me to play. One of the residents suggested a song by Gospel Artist Jeffrey Majors called "Psalms 23". I was so excited to listen to it. I played the song from a music app on my phone, and we began to worship GOD. The presence of the Holy Spirit began to fill the room, and we praised GOD with the fruit of our lips. Oh Immanuel, GOD is truly with us!

BEFORE THE THRONE

There's something special about being before your throne

All of life's cares and sorrows seem to melt away, and it's you and me alone

There is no shame because you know me through and through

I'm simply your daughter, kneeling before her FATHER, feeling honored to know you.

Before your throne, I'm not what my enemies have called me

But I stand in your presence knowing my true identity

So, I lay the issues of my heart before your feet

Being fully persuaded that the enemy will not triumph over me

The strength I need to live, and the peace you promised to provide

I find in the secret place, of the MOST HIGH

My soul thirsts and hungers after you, only you can satisfy

The desire to be before your throne, 'til the sweet by and by

WORDS OF WISDOM

BEFORE THE THRONE

It is a privilege and honor to go before the Throne of GOD. The word of GOD says in 2Chronicle 7:14

If my people, which are called by my name, shall humble themselves, and pray, and seek my face, and turn from their wicked ways; then will I hear from heaven, and will forgive their sin, and will heal their land.

To know that GOD hears us from HIS throne and answers by HIS word is powerful in itself! Let us not take for granted the opportunity to seek our Heavenly Father through prayer, for the answers and guidance that we so desperately need. Let us not walk in self-righteousness or pride, believing that we know what to do, or how to respond to the issues of life. Only GOD is all knowing and all seeing. Allow HIM to guide you in the direction you should go. Sometimes HE may lead you down a path that you may not be familiar with. Just know that you are never alone, and that HIS ways are perfect. AMEN

ROYALTY

Oh, how great is our loving Father, who has made us royal

No longer are we clothed in our sins, but in fine linen.

We walk in HIS courts daily as HIS royal representatives

We worship HIM in Spirit and in truth, with no shame within

Yes, we are royal, let us live as such

By the renewing of our minds, we can see ourselves as we truly are

Royalty, a peculiar people, a royal priesthood of the Most High GOD

Ambassadors for a kingdom that is soon to come, and a High Priest destined to reign forever

So, prepare your hearts to receive this truth

Embrace this reality, and the royalty within you

WORDS OF WISDOM

ROYALTY

The Holy Spirit led me to Zechariah Chapter 3. The story is about a high priest name Joshua, standing before the LORD, and satan being present to resist the promises of GOD upon his life. The LORD rebuked satan, and blessed Joshua with fresh garments and a new turban for his head. This particular turban was given to those from the royal family or from the priesthood.

Reading this story reminded me of 1Peter 2:9 that says "But you are a chosen generation, a royal priesthood, a holy nation, a peculiar people; that ye should show forth the praises of him who hath called you out of darkness into his marvelous light;"

When we dedicate our lives to the Lord Jesus Christ, we are engrafted into the "Royal Priesthood". God in HIS great mercy, called us out of darkness, pain, and the temptations of this world, to show forth HIS new creation within us. We are called to be ambassadors of HIS kingdom on earth. We must learn to walk and live our lives, knowing that we are a part of HIS royal priesthood. Do not allow your pass hurts and failures, to hinder you from your true identity in Christ Jesus. Do not allow your current circumstances to determine your future. Renew your mind by reading and meditating on the Word of God and allow it to tell you who you really are! You my brother in Christ, yes you my sister in Christ, are ROYALTY!

KING OF GLORY

For so long I could not see

That the King of Glory was always with me

Blinded by sin and the pleasures of this world

Living as if I was a woman, but in reality, I was a broken little girl

Finally, I reached the place of desperation

Ready for change I embarked on my journey of separation

From the torment of the enemy that plagued me for years

It was time for me to face my fears

I wouldn't face them alone, cause I could finally see

That the King of Glory was right there with me

WORDS OF WISDOM

KING OF GLORY

Lift up your heads, O you gates! And be lifted up, you everlasting doors! And the King of glory shall come in. Who is this King of glory? The LORD strong and mighty, The LORD mighty in battle. Lift up your heads, O you gates! Lift up, you everlasting doors! And the King of glory shall come in. Who is this King of glory? The LORD of hosts, HE is the King of glory. Selah (Psalms 24:7-10) NKJV

Many of us have experienced pain and sorrow. We know that GOD is our healer, but sometimes the sorrow can weigh us down. When we make the decision to lift up our heads and cry to the LORD, HE is faithful to come to our rescue. Yes, HE knew that you would be facing this crisis. Yes, HE knew that it may cause pain, and disrupt your life, and yes, HE does care. The LORD encourages us in 2Corithians 4:17 that,

"For our light affliction, which is but for a moment, is working for us a far more exceeding and eternal weight of glory, while we do not look at the things which are seen, but at the things which are not seen. For the things which are seen are temporary, but the things which are not seen are eternal."

What is this scripture saying to us? Simply put, there is purpose in our pain! The word of GOD encourages us to take our focus off of what we see and how we feel, and to focus on HIM! The storm is temporary, and it will pass over, but GOD's glory from it is eternal! GOD knew that the storms of life would impact us in various ways. The key is to allow the storms to make us better, and not bitter.

How are you responding to your current circumstances? Are you seeking solace and comfort in the world, or in the loving arms of the Lord Jesus Christ? In the midst of your pain and sorrow, make the decision to lift up your head and cry out to the LORD. He has promised that HE would comfort us. HIS ears are tentatively listening, and HE hears the cry of HIS people. Your circumstances may not change immediately, but by faith, you are changed for the better by your circumstances. AMEN

LOVE SAID…

NO, Said Love, I don't condemn you for your sins, Repent!! Pick up your cross and follow me

GO, Said Love, and walk out your salvation in fear and trembling before me

SHOW, Said Love, how my mercy and lovingkindness has saved you

LOVE Said NO

LOVE Said GO

LOVE Said SHOW

Show, the world you are a new creation in Christ Jesus

Go, and declare the Gospel of the Kingdom throughout the nations

NO, I will never leave you nor forsake you[3]

LOVE Said NO, GO, SHOW, the world that I AM

1. Hebrews 13:5 (New Kings James Version)

TESTIMONY

LOVE SAID…

I was praying to the LORD one particular morning to inspire and give me creativity about what to write, when I suddenly heard the Holy Spirit say, "LOVE SAID" The Holy Spirit began to give me the words to this poem, and as I wrote it down, I realized that this was the Great Commission from

Mathew 28: 18-20!

And Jesus came and spoke unto them , saying, All power is given unto me in heaven and in earth. Go ye therefore, and teach all nations, baptizing them in the name of the Father, and of the Son, and of the Holy Ghost; Teaching them to observe all things whatsoever I have commanded you: and lo, I am with you always, even unto the end of the world. Amen.

We all have been called to share the gospel of the kingdom of GOD. We must learn to say No to the lies and temptations of the enemy, Go and be a witness for Christ, and Show how good the LORD truly is! HALLELUJAH.

LOVING YOU IS LIKE….

Loving you is like a gentle breeze caressing my skin on a hot summer day,

Beautiful, Gentle and Refreshing to my soul

Loving you is like my momma's sweet potato pies; addictive, Oh taste and see that the LORD is good[4]: Blessed is the man who trusts in the LORD And whose hope is the LORD.[5] For in doing so, we can expect HIS goodness always, just like momma's sweet potato pies!

Loving you is like standing at a bus stop during a thunderstorm but wearing a raincoat; no matter how bad the storm, I'm covered and protected, safe in your arms.

Loving you is like cuddling my favorite teddy bear; it comforts me, gives me rest, and brings a smile to my face.

Loving you is like watching the beauty and splendor of sunrise; like the sun, you chase away the darkness, and fill the earth with your glory. As the sun, your light gives life to everything it touches.

For you have given me life, and loving you is my life.

Psalms 34:8 (New King James Version)

Jeremiah 17:7 (New King James Version)

TESTIMONY

LOVING YOU IS LIKE…

My biological father was not in my life. My stepfather loved us (me and my four brothers) but because of his struggles with addiction and alcohol, he wasn't consistently a good example of what it meant to be a father. As a teenager, I went into the world broken, and I found myself in broken relationships. I later discovered that I wasn't looking for a boyfriend, but a Father!

When I re-dedicated my life to the Lord Jesus Christ, HE walked me through the healing process as a loving Father. A Father that was patient, faithful, protective, and encouraging. HE gave me rest for my soul, and strength to endure the painful process of forgiveness and healing.

Finally, the revelation of GOD's love found a place in my heart, and it changed my life forever. I was searching for something that I always had, which was

HIM. Loving HIM is like nothing I can ever express with words, but HE understands perfectly.

HAVE MERCY ON ME LORD!

Forgive me Father, I have sinned

Even though I promised I wouldn't do it again

The temptations of this world, I can't always withstand

Now I know in a greater way, that I need your

Almighty Hand

To keep me from doing the things I should not

And to lead me away from the enemy's plots

So, hear my cry, and be attentive to my plea

Stretch out your loving hands and have mercy on me.

WORDS OF WISDOM

HAVE MERCY ON ME LORD!

On this journey with Christ, we will make mistakes. The key is to repent, get back up, and keep walking. The word of GOD says that there is no condemnation in Christ Jesus (See Romans 1:17).

I want to encourage you to keep walking, keep striving, and believing that GOD's grace and mercy is plentiful. Be grateful for HIS grace and mercy, but do NOT use it as a pass to commit sin willfully and knowingly. By doing so, the very purpose for Christ coming into the world would be in vain!

It's only in your personal relationship with the Lord Jesus Christ, that will enable you to stand against the temptations of the enemy. Make time to read the word of GOD and seek the face of the LORD through prayer and fasting for more of HIS Spirit. GOD has already made a way of escape for you! Seek HIM for your complete deliverance. THE VICTORY IS ALREADY YOURS, now walk it out!

CLOTHED IN HIS GLORY

It makes no difference to me

That my bracelet didn't come from Tiffany's

And that the shoes on my feet

Originally did not belong to me

For I am clothed in HIS GLORY

Nope, there is no shame

That my cute dress has no famous name

Or that my nails were bought at a pharmacy

I dare to be unique, and I'm finally ok with me

Cause I'm clothed in HIS GLORY

My beauty can't be replicated by you

And there's nobody for me to apologize to

For being the beautiful creation GOD made me to be

For so many years I was blind, but now I can finally see

That I'm clothed in HIS GLORY

TESTIMONY

CLOTHED IN HIS GLORY

A few years ago, my finances was under extreme attack. No matter how frugal I lived, it was as if I had holes in my pockets! So much so that I couldn't afford to buy food, clothes, or the basic essentials for everyday living. Thank GOD for the Food Pantry at my church, and other community resources that helped me during that season of my life.

As I reflect on that season, I think about the "one thing" that I esteemed to mean so much, that GOD allowed to be taken away from me because I couldn't afford to buy it: Clothes. I love fashion and costume jewelry, and I know that there's nothing wrong with that. The issue was attaching my identity to it. GOD allowed me to walk through that season to reveal the vanity in my heart, and to teach me that my identity was not in "what" I have but in "who" I am!

Do not allow society to tell you that if you don't look a certain way, or because you don't live a certain lifestyle, that you have no value, or that you are not beautiful. Do not allow society to mold you into "its distorted image" of what beauty, success, and identity is. We belong to Jesus Christ. In HIM we all are fearfully and wonderfully made! (See Psalms 139:14)

"Our Beauty in Christ: PRICELESS"

ONLY TIME WILL TELL

Time will truly tell

If the word of GOD is real, or some poor man's fairytale

To encourage him to believe,

Beyond what he could currently see

Only time will tell

If there is another life beyond this veil

And that finality doesn't end on earth, but before the throne of GOD

Time will truly tell

If the prophecies written long ago are true

That there is a real battle for your heart, and who will rule over you

Time surely will tell

If we are ready to fight the good fight of faith

Believing in the power of HIS blood,

And in HIM we are perfectly safe

Only time will tell

WORDS OF WISDOM
ONLY TIME WILL TELL

The word of GOD says in John 16:33(KJV)

"These things I have spoken unto you, that in me ye might have peace. In the world ye shall have tribulation: but be of good cheer; I have overcome the world. "

It's time. It's time for the LORD to manifest HIS GLORY. Many do not believe that HE exists, but now is the time for HIM to prove them wrong. Let us position ourselves to be witnesses of HIS goodness towards humanity. Yes, as believers in Christ we may suffer for HIS name sake, but HE has promised us victory over all the works of the enemy.

"LET GOD ARISE, AND HIS ENEMIES BE SCATTERED"

(Psalms 68 KJV, emphasis are mines)

AN OVERCOMERS DECREE

FATHER GOD in the name of the Lord Jesus Christ we thank you. We thank you LORD GOD for who you are. Your grace and mercy endures forever. We thank you LORD GOD for your Son, Jesus Christ of Nazareth, who came to this earth to redeem us from the hands of the enemy. We are more than conquerors because HE chose to lay down HIS life. No man took it from HIM. We thank you LORD GOD that we can now live, move, and have our being in you, because of HIS victory on the cross.

So, we shout "GLORY, GLORY, GLORY TO THE LAMB GOD. We renounce every spirit of fear, doubt, anxiety, hopelessness, helplessness, poverty, defeat, sickness, disease, and infirmity in the mighty name of Jesus Christ. We declare and decree the living word of GOD, that HIS promises are yes and amen. (2Cor 1:20) We declare and decree that our past is behind us, our future is before us, and GOD is with us. We declare and decree that we are not weak, feeble or without help. For your word has declared that we are overcomers by the blood of the Lamb and the words of our testimonies.(Rev 12:11) We declare and decree that we are the head and not the tale, above and never beneath.   (Deuteronomy 28:13).

We thank you right now LORD GOD that no weapon formed against us will prosper, it won't stand, it won't overtake, it won't destroy us in the name of the Lord Jesus Christ. We praise you Heavenly Father, that you said we can do all things through Christ who strengthens us (Phil 4:13). Therefore, we are able to forgive our enemies, renounce all negative thoughts, emotions, and actions. We can lift up our voices and declare the goodness of the Lord. We can share our testimonies without fear, shame, and condemnation, because we know that GOD is with us.

We declare this decree by faith, that we are fearfully and wonderfully made, (Psalms 139:14). We are beautiful, strong, confident, smart, and filled with the anointing of GOD, to unapologetically represent the Kingdom of GOD on earth. Our demographics do not matter. Our social classes do not matter. For we all are royalty through Christ Jesus. We are rich in HIS blessings and favor. We are covered by HIS blood. We have experienced HIS Resurrection power, during the darkest hours of our lives. We are not slaves to our emotions, but are renewed in spirit and mind, because we have the mind of Christ.

We declare and decree that we will no longer hold our heads down in shame, embarrassment, or fear, but we will lift our heads in confidence in who we are in Christ. We thank you Blessed One, for giving us the opportunity to reflect you on this earth, and that our lives will bring you glory. Eye hath not seen, nor ear heard, neither have entered into the heart of man, the things which God hath prepared for them that love HIM. (1Cor 2:9) In Jesus Christ glorious and mighty name we make this declaration and decree, AMEN.

FINAL TAKE AWAYS

GOD has the power to turn our mess into a message. After reading this book, I pray that you consider the following…

1. GOD luvs you. Do not allow the enemy to make you doubt GOD's luv for you. Yes, you may be experiencing pain or frustration in your life, but GOD is right there with you. HE promised in His word that HE will never leave you or forsake you (See Deuteronomy 31:6). HE luvs you so much that HE gave HIS ONLY SON, to carry your burdens and sorrows, so that you can experience real joy, peace, and HIS unconditional luv for you. Again, GOD will never leave you. HE is right there with you.

2. There's purpose in your pain. When you are frustrated, confused, and fearful it's difficult to see purpose. All you feel is pain, doubt, and a longing for escape. The very thing that the enemy tries to use against you, GOD has the amazing ability to turn into purpose. Most often, GOD uses your brokenness to encourage and bless others facing similar situations. As others around you are blessed by your sharing, whether its words of encouragement or some physical/monetary assistance, it empowers you to continue in your giving, and purpose comes forth. Do not be ashamed to share your journey with others, because in doing so your purpose and destiny will be revealed.

3. Your attitude matters. When going through hard times, it's difficult to have a positive attitude. However, maintaining a positive attitude is everything! Why should you strive to have a positive attitude? Because GOD wants us to believe that HE has already given you the victory! HE wants you to have confidence in HIS ability to fight your battles, and although it may be painful, HE has ordained for you to be an overcomer! Believe in HIM and rejoice in what GOD is doing in your life.

4. Your Identity is in Christ, not people. People are searching for purpose and identity. Society pushes a belief that identity is found in financial status, race, culture, and sexual orientation. This is not so for believers of Christ. The word of GOD tells us in 1Peter 2:9 "But you are a chosen people, a royal priesthood, a holy nation, GOD's special possession, that you may declare the praises of him who called you out of darkness into his marvelous light." NIV. Do not allow people to make you feel inferior, unworthy, or incapable of being who you are in Christ. Develop your personal relationship with the LORD. Seek HIM through the word of GOD, prayer, and worship, and He will reveal your purpose and identity to you. You are unique, and wonderfully made! GOD created you to do something only you are gifted and anointed to do. Learn to be ok with being different and choose to reflect GOD and not people.

5. Don't be embarrassed to share your story. Do not allow anyone to make you feel guilty or condemn you about your past. When you give your life to Jesus Christ, all of your sins are removed. When we wash our natural bodies, the water and soap cleanses us and removes all the dirt from us. In the spirit realm, the blood of Jesus Christ and the Holy Spirit cleanses our spiritual bodies and as a result, the dirt and stains of our sins are removed. I encourage you to embrace the new person GOD has created you to be. Rejoice in the freedom and peace the LORD has given you. Don't be ashamed of what GOD has delivered you from. Share your story and watch how GOD uses it to bring hope, deliverance, and joy to others.

 # ABOUT THE AUTHOR

Hidden Diamond is a native of Atlanta, GA with a passion to see the Glory of GOD manifested in the lives of GOD's people. Enough said.

Hidden Diamond

Book References

New King James Version,

Psalms 34:8, Psalms 91, Psalms 42:1-2, Psalms 23,
Deuteronomy 31:8, Hebrews 11:4, John 8:36

King James Version

Psalms 68, John 16:33, Romans 1:17, Matthew 28:18-
20, 2Corithians 4:17, 1Peter 2:9, Zechariah 3
2Corithians 7:14, Zechariah 4:6, Psalms 65:6,
Philippians 4:13. Psalms 24:7-10, Isaiah 40:31, Psalms
150:6

 NOTES

 NOTES

 NOTES

NOTES

 NOTES

 NOTES

NOTES

NOTES

Printed in the USA
CPSIA information can be obtained
at www.ICGtesting.com
LVHW020825030924
789973LV00003B/27